C000141015

A CULINARY JOURNEY

Exploring destinations and discovering different cultures and traditions is at the heart of every Viking journey. And of course food – not only the recipes prepared by our onboard chefs, but also local cuisine in all the fascinating places our ships visit – is an essential part of the overall Viking experience.

We hope this book helps you to recreate the flavors of your travels back home in your own kitchen, and inspires you to continue exploring the world.

ASIA & AUSTRALASIA

Asia is home to many cultures, all with their own distinctive cuisine. Even rice comes in many different varieties – jasmine rice, for example, is found across southeast Asia, including Vietnam and Cambodia, while long-grain rice is widely eaten in China. Some ingredients are common to many cultures in eastern and southeast Asia, including ginger, garlic, chilies, soy and tofu. Chinese cuisine originated over 4,000 years ago in what is known as the Eight Great Traditions, including the native cooking styles of Hunan and Sichuan provinces, known for their bold flavors. Vietnamese recipes use a wide range of herbs, including lemongrass, mint and cilantro, while Cambodian cuisine includes tropical fruits. Meanwhile, seafood is popular in Japan, where it is often served raw.

CHINA &
HONG KONG

Cosmopolitan Shanghai, imperial
Beijing and the legendary Yangtze
River – China is one of the most
remarkable countries, and its cuisine
is equally extraordinary and incredibly
varied. Hong Kong's position as an
international port ensures a similarly
diverse range of delicious food.

SWEET AND SOUR PORK

Serves 4

Oil for frying
1 lb (450g) pork loin,
   cubed
1 clove garlic, chopped
1 tsp fresh ginger
1 red bell pepper,
   deseeded and chopped
1 green bell pepper,
   deseeded and chopped
1 bunch scallions (spring
   onions), white part
3 ½ oz (100g) pineapple,
   chopped
1 tbsp tomato purée
1 tbsp plum sauce
1 tbsp Worcestershire
   sauce
1 tbsp Chinese rice wine
   vinegar
1 tbsp oyster sauce
1 tbsp honey
2 tbsp pineapple juice

FOR THE MARINADE:
1 tsp soy sauce
½ tsp cornstarch
   (cornflour)
1 tsp Chinese rice wine

1 Mix together the marinade ingredients and stir in the pork. Allow to marinate for half an hour, mixing occasionally.

2 Heat the oil in a large, heavy-based frying pan and fry the pork until golden brown, then remove and set aside.

3 Grate the fresh ginger and then add it, along with the garlic, to the pan and fry briefly. Add the chopped peppers and scallions and cook until softened, then add the pineapple pieces and finally the pork.

4 In a bowl, mix together the tomato purée, plum sauce, Worcestershire sauce, rice wine vinegar, oyster sauce, honey and pineapple juice, then pour into the pan. Cook just until the sauce thickens then serve immediately with rice or noodles.

POT STICKERS

Makes 20 dumplings

9 oz (250g) minced pork or chicken

2 scallions (spring onions) finely chopped

1 oz (30g) tinned bamboo shoots, finely chopped

1 tsp fresh ginger, grated

1 tbsp cornstarch (cornflour)

Pinch of white pepper

2 tsp soy sauce

1 pack round Chinese dumpling wrappers

2 tbsp vegetable oil

5 fl oz (150ml) water

FOR THE DIPPING SAUCE:

6 tbsp soy sauce

4 tbsp Chinese black vinegar or balsamic vinegar

2 tbsp sesame oil

2 tbsp chili garlic sauce

1 In a bowl, mix the pork with the scallions, bamboo shoots and ginger. Sprinkle over the cornstarch and pepper and mix thoroughly, then stir in the soy sauce.

2 Place a tablespoon of the pork mixture in the center of each dumpling wrapper, brush the edges with water, fold in half and press against the edges to seal, pressing lightly down to form a flat bottom.

3 Heat a large, heavy-based frying pan and add a tablespoon of oil. Add half of the pot stickers and cook for 3 to 5 minutes until the bottoms are golden brown. Add half the water, cover and reduce the heat, steaming for another 3 to 5 minutes until all the water is absorbed. Transfer the cooked dumplings to a warm plate, and then repeat the frying and steaming process with the remaining pot stickers.

4 Mix all the dipping sauce ingredients together and serve immediately with the hot pot stickers.

HONG KONG FRIED RICE

Serves 4

2 oz (55g) frozen peas
1 carrot, diced
1 tbsp rapeseed oil
1 onion, finely chopped
6 oz (170g) large
   shrimp/prawns peeled,
   deveined and chopped
1 lb (450g) cooked
   long-grain rice
4 oz (115g) cooked
   ham, chopped
2 eggs, beaten
1 tsp salt
1 tbsp soy sauce
3 tbsp ketchup

1 Blanch the peas and carrots in boiling, salted water until just tender, then drain and set aside.
2 Heat the wok until smoking, then add in the oil. Stir fry the onion until soft, then add in the shrimp. Cook for a couple more minutes until the shrimp are just pink.
3 Add in the cooked rice, ham and vegetables, then pour over the beaten egg. Finally sprinkle with salt and stir in the soy sauce and ketchup. Stir fry for another two minutes, and then serve immediately.

CANTONESE SHRIMP AND SCALLOP STIR FRY

Serves 4

4 tbsp rapeseed oil

4 garlic cloves, finely chopped

1 red chili pepper, sliced diagonally

Thumb sized piece fresh ginger, peeled and finely chopped

2 tbsp Shaoxing rice wine

12 large shrimp/prawns peeled and deveined

6 fresh scallops, halved Salt and freshly ground black pepper

2 scallions (spring onions), sliced diagonally

3 oz (85g) snow peas (mangetout)

2 bok choy (pak choi), quartered

1-2 tbsp light soy sauce, to taste

1 tsp sesame oil

1 Place the wok on a high heat. When it starts to smoke, add in the rapeseed oil along with the garlic, chili and ginger. Cook for one minute, then add in the rice wine.

2 Add in the prawns and cook for a further minute, keeping everything moving in the wok.

3 Season the scallop halves with salt and pepper, then add in to the wok.

4 Add in the vegetables along with a splash of water to create some steam. Cook for two to three minutes or until the vegetables have just started to wilt.

5 Season with the soy sauce, then serve straight away with steamed jasmine rice. Drizzle with a little sesame oil.

VIETNAM

From the extraordinary Mekong River to its fascinating cities, Vietnam is utterly compelling. The French influence on Vietnamese cuisine means that there is a proliferation of bakeries in Ho Chi Minh City and Hanoi, as well as street food.

BEEF PHỞ

Serves 4

3 pints (1.4 liters) veal or
   beef stock
1 onion, chopped
2 whole star anise
½ cinnamon stick
1 clove
½ tsp whole
   peppercorns
1 thick slice fresh ginger
2 tsp sugar
1 tsp salt
1 tsp fish sauce
1 pack flat rice noodles
9 oz (250g) sirloin steak

TO GARNISH:
Sriracha (Vietnamese
   hot chili sauce)
Hoisin sauce
1 onion, thinly sliced
Fresh cilantro
   (coriander), chopped
Bean sprouts
Sweet Thai basil leaves
Thinly sliced scallions
   (spring onions)
Limes, quartered

1 Make the aromatic broth by heating the stock in a saucepan and adding in the onion, star anise, cinnamon stick, clove, peppercorns, ginger, sugar, salt and fish sauce. Allow to simmer for at least 30 minutes, then strain and return to the pan, discarding the spices.
2 Meanwhile, cook the rice noodles until soft, according to packet instructions.
3 Slice the steak as thinly as possible, then place some noodles into each bowl, and top with a few raw beef slices. Ladle the boiling broth over the beef and noodles and serve with the garnishes and sauces.

VIETNAMESE FRESH SUMMER ROLLS

Makes 8 rolls

1 pack pad Thai rice
   noodles
8 rice paper wrappers
24 medium shrimp,
   cooked
1 bunch mint
1 bunch cilantro
   (coriander)
2 or 3 Thai basil
   stems
1 carrot, peeled
   and sliced into fine
   matchsticks
½ cucumber, deseeded
   and sliced into fine
   matchsticks
Shredded lettuce
4 tbsp salted peanuts,
   chopped

FOR THE DIPPING
SAUCE:
1 tbsp sugar
Juice of 1 lime
1 tbsp fish sauce
1 garlic clove, crushed
1 small red chili,
   deseeded and finely
   chopped

1 Cook the rice noodles according to the pack
instructions, drain and reserve. Assemble all the
filling ingredients and pick the herb leaves from
the stalks. Make sure you have a bowl of cold
water handy for the rice paper wrappers.
2 To assemble the rolls, soak each rice paper
wrapper until it's pliable, then spread flat onto a
chopping board. Arrange three shrimp into the
center, then layer up with the mint, cilantro,
carrot, cucumber and lettuce. Add a small
handful of the rice noodles, then finally scatter
over some of the chopped peanuts.
3 Fold the bottom of the roll up over the
ingredients, flap in the sides and then roll up
into a neat parcel.
4 To make the dipping sauce, whisk all the
ingredients together until the sugar has
dissolved. Serve with the summer rolls.

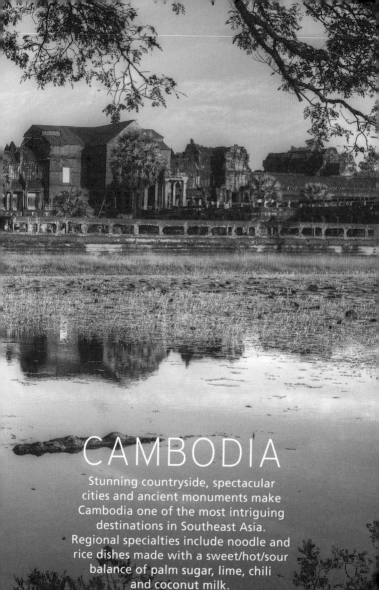

CAMBODIA

Stunning countryside, spectacular
cities and ancient monuments make
Cambodia one of the most intriguing
destinations in Southeast Asia.
Regional specialties include noodle and
rice dishes made with a sweet/hot/sour
balance of palm sugar, lime, chili
and coconut milk.

KHMER RED CHICKEN CURRY

Serves 4

1 lemongrass stalk,
  chopped
1 tbsp turmeric
2 tbsp fresh ginger,
  grated
2 kaffir lime leaves
6 cloves of garlic,
  chopped
1 red chili, deseeded
  and chopped
1 shallot, peeled and
  chopped
2 tbsp oil
1 lb (450g) chicken,
  either breast, leg or
  thigh meat
2 tbsp sugar
1 tbsp fish sauce
2 sweet potatoes,
  peeled and chopped
1 carrot, chopped
1 potato, chopped
4 star anise
7 oz (200g) tinned
  coconut milk
Pinch salt
1 lime

1 To make the aromatic paste, pound the lemongrass, turmeric, ginger, lime leaves, garlic, chili and shallot together until they make a smooth paste.

2 Heat the oil in a heavy-based saucepan or wok and fry the curry paste for 1 to 2 minutes. Add the chicken, then the sugar and fish sauce. Fry until the chicken is opaque, and then add the vegetables.

3 Next, pour over the coconut milk, and add a pinch of salt, the star anise and a splash of water. Simmer until the chicken is cooked through and the vegetables are tender. Before serving, add a squeeze of lime and serve with steamed rice or crisp slices of baguette.

BAI SACH CHROUK

Serves 4

14 oz (400g) lean pork
  loin, thinly sliced

FOR THE MARINADE:

3 garlic cloves, crushed

2 tbsp soy sauce

2 oz (55g) grated palm
  sugar, or light
  brown sugar

7 oz (200g) tinned
  coconut milk

2 tbsp fish sauce

1 lime, juiced

FOR THE PICKLES:

2-3 carrots, grated

½ cucumber, cut into
  thin strips

Handful of fresh cilantro
  (coriander) leaves

1 tsp salt

3 ½ oz (100g) sugar

4 fl oz (120ml) white
  vinegar

4 fl oz (120ml) water

1 First, make the marinade by combining all the ingredients together. Add the pork, cover and allow it to marinate for a few hours, ideally leaving it overnight.

2 To make the pickles, grate the carrots and cut the cucumber into thin strips, then combine the rest of the ingredients and pour over the vegetables. Add in the cilantro, stir well, then cover and leave for at least an hour (it will keep for a couple of weeks refrigerated).

3 Remove the pork from the marinade and either grill or barbecue until well caramelized and completely cooked through. Serve with steamed white rice and the pickled vegetables.

SINGAPORE

Given its position as an international
seaport, it is no surprise that
Singaporean cuisine relies heavily on
seafood. Malay, Chinese and Indian
traditions all contribute, and food plays
a crucial role in defining national
and cultural identity.

SINGAPORE CHILI CRAB

Serves 4

FOR THE SPICE PASTE:

2-3 shallots, peeled and
   roughly chopped

3 garlic cloves

1 thumb-sized piece
   ginger, chopped

3 red chilies

1 tsp shrimp paste

FOR THE CRAB:

1 hard shell crab,
   cooked, cleaned and
   cut into pieces

2 tbsp rapeseed oil

2 tbsp palm sugar

4 tbsp tomato ketchup

2 tbsp soy sauce

TO GARNISH:

1 red chili, sliced

Cilantro (coriander),
   leaves only

2 scallions (spring
   onions) sliced

1 To make the spice paste, place all the ingredients in a small food processor and blend until smooth, then set aside.

2 Prepare the crab: remove the shell, detach and crack the legs and claws, discard the dead man's fingers then chop the body into four pieces.

3 In a wok or a large frying pan, heat the oil until smoking, then cook the spice paste for one to two minutes. Add in the crab and stir fry to coat in the paste, then add the palm sugar, ketchup and soy sauce.

4 Cook for five to six minutes or until the crab is heated through. Serve garnished with the chili, cilantro and scallions, with rice or steamed buns.

HOKKIEN HAE MEE

Serves 4

1 lb (450g) whole fresh
shrimp

4 tbsp vegetable oil

6 oz (170g) pork belly

1 lb (450g) pork spare
ribs

Large pinch salt

1 tbsp palm sugar

2 cloves garlic, smashed

2 tsp fish sauce

1 tsp soy sauce

3 oz (85g) bean sprouts

7 oz (200g) fresh egg
noodles

TO GARNISH:

1 red chili, sliced

1 lime, quartered

1 Shell the shrimp, reserving the heads and shells. Rinse and set aside.

2 Heat a wok or a large saucepan. When it starts smoking, pour in 3 tbsp oil and add the shrimp heads and shells. Stir fry until they turn bright red. Then set aside.

3 In a large saucepan, cover the pork belly and spare ribs with water. Add the palm sugar and smashed garlic. Bring to the boil, then reduce the heat and simmer for around 30 minutes, or until the pork is cooked through.

4 Remove the pork with a slotted spoon. When cool enough to handle, shred the meat from the ribs and slice the pork belly then set aside.

5 To make the stock, add the reserved prawn heads and shells to the pork cooking water, then boil for one hour, skimming occasionally. Strain through a fine sieve, and season with the fish sauce and soy sauce.

6 Pour the broth into a fresh saucepan, bring to the boil, then add in the raw prawns. Cook for around 30 seconds, then remove and set aside.

7 To assemble the dish, add the noodles and bean sprouts into the broth, along with the prawns and pork. When everything is heated through, transfer into bowls and serve, garnished with fresh chili and lime.

JAPAN

Japanese cuisine, and in particular its
sushi, is celebrated around the world.
Much of Japanese food is accompanied
by rice or noodles, and specialties
include miso soup and *tempura*
(vegetables fried in a light batter).
Seafood is prominent, and often
served raw as sushi or sashimi.

TEMAKI SUSHI

Serves 4

7oz (200g) sushi rice
2 fl oz (60ml) rice
   vinegar
1 tbsp sugar
½ tsp salt
1 pack sushi nori sheets

FOR THE FILLINGS:
Sushi grade fresh tuna
Salmon roe
Teriyaki chicken
Avocado
Cucumber
Shrimp
Wasabi
Sushi ginger

1 Cook the rice according to the packet instructions. Mix the rice vinegar, sugar and salt and stir through the rice. Allow to cool.

2 Cut the nori sheets in half and assemble all the fillings, cut into small 4 inch (10cm) strips.

3 To assemble the temaki, spread a layer of rice over each nori sheet, then add fillings to taste. Roll into a cone shape, and moisten one edge before pressing to seal.

MISO NIKOMI UDON

Serves 2

30 fl oz (890ml) dashi
  stock
4 tbsp miso paste
2 tsp sake
1 tsp sugar
4 oz (115g) chicken
  thigh or leg meat
1 piece abura-age (fried
  tofu)
8 oz (225g) udon
  noodles, ready to serve
  or cooked according to
  pack instructions
4 scallions (spring
  onions), sliced

1 Pour the dashi stock into a large saucepan and bring to the boil. Remove a little of the liquid in a small jug, then stir in the miso paste until dissolved. Add back in to the stock.

2 Add the sake and sugar to the broth, then add in the chicken. Simmer gently until the chicken is cooked through.

3 Pour boiling water over the abura-age, then cut into strips. Add into the broth along with the noodles and scallions (reserve a few for a garnish). Simmer for five minutes to allow all the flavors to combine, then serve in bowls, garnished with the reserved scallions.

INDONESIA

The volcanic island of Bali has a rich culinary heritage. Rice is the staple grain, and accompanies meat, seafood and vegetables. Tropical fruits are also abundant, and street vendors specialize in local delicacies. Hinduism is widely followed here, and ornate dishes are created for religious festivals.

NASI GORENG

Serves 4

3 tbsp vegetable oil

4 large eggs, beaten

7 oz (200g) shallots,
  thinly sliced

2 cloves garlic, minced

1 lemongrass stalk,
  outer leaves removed,
  finely chopped

Thumb sized piece fresh
  ginger, peeled and
  finely chopped

1 tsp shrimp paste

2 tsp tamarind paste

2 red bird's eye chilies

2 chicken breasts,
  chopped

12 large shrimp (prawns),
  peeled and deveined

1 medium carrot, sliced

1lb (450g) cooked long
  grain rice

2 tbsp kecap manis
  (sweet soy sauce)

1 tbsp light soy sauce

TO GARNISH:

½ cucumber, deseeded
  and thinly sliced

4 scallions (spring
  onions), sliced

1 Heat one tablespoon of the oil in a large, heavy-based frying pan and pour in the egg. Gently pull the edges into the center, allowing the uncooked egg to reach the heat of the pan, until the omelette is just cooked through. Flip the outer thirds into the middle, slice thinly and transfer to a plate to keep warm.

2 Heat a wok or large frying pan until smoking then pour in the remaining oil. Add in the shallots, garlic, lemongrass, ginger, shrimp paste, tamarind paste and sliced chilies and stir fry for two to three minutes.

3 Add in the chicken, shrimp and carrot, stir frying until cooked through. Finally, add in the rice along with the kecap manis, soy sauce and the shredded omelette. Garnish with the cucumber and scallions and serve immediately.

PAN-FRIED CHICKEN
WITH BALINESE SAMBAL MATAH

Serves 4

4 boneless chicken
   breasts
1 tbsp all purpose
   (plain) flour
Salt and pepper
2 tbsp oil

FOR THE SAMBAL
MATAH:

2 stems lemongrass,
   thinly sliced
6 shallots, thinly sliced
4 red bird's eye chilies,
   thinly sliced
1 tbsp coconut oil
1 tsp shrimp paste
½ tsp sugar
½ tsp salt
1 lime, juice only

1 Remove the skin from the chicken breast, season the flour with the salt and pepper and dust each breast lightly in the seasoned flour.
2 Heat the oil in a heavy based frying pan and fry the chicken until golden (around 6 to 8 minutes), then turn and repeat on the other side, making sure it's cooked through. Remove from the pan and allow to cool, then shred the chicken into small pieces.
3 To make the sambal matah, combine the lemongrass, shallots and chilies in a bowl. Stir in the warmed coconut oil and the shrimp paste. Then season to taste with the sugar, salt and lime juice.
4 Toss the sambal matah through the shredded chicken and serve with steamed white rice.

AUSTRALIA

Aboriginal food was traditionally based
on hunting and gathering, and little
of this was embraced by incomers.
But today the region is famed for its
multicultural menus. Native foods like
kangaroo, crocodile, macadamia nuts
and yams are widespread. With seafood
and meat still the star attraction, the
nation's dedication to barbecuing is
renowned worldwide.

SALT AND PEPPER SQUID

Serves 4

Vegetable oil, for frying
1 lb (450g) small squid, cleaned
1 tbsp black peppercorns
1 tbsp Szechuan peppercorns
1 tsp sea salt
4 tbsp all purpose (plain) flour
4 tbsp cornstarch (cornflour)

FOR THE GARNISH:
1 red chili, deseeded and sliced
2 scallions (spring onions), sliced
1 clove garlic, sliced

1 Half fill a large pan (or deep fat fryer) with the oil and allow to come up to 350°F (180°C).

2 If you're using whole squid, separate the tentacles and remove the clear 'quill'. Discard the heads and then cut the hoods into 1cm rings. Set aside.

3 Crush the peppercorns, then mix with the flour and cornstarch.

4 Toss the squid pieces in the flour mixture, making sure they're well covered, then transfer to the fryer. Fry in batches until golden (about 1-1 ½ minutes), then remove and drain on some kitchen paper.

5 Make the garnish by briefly frying the chili, scallions and garlic in a little oil, taking care not to burn the garlic.

6 Serve the squid rings immediately, scattered with the garnish.

BARBEQUED SHRIMP
WITH MEXICAN PICO DE GALLO

Serves 4 as an appetizer

16 large fresh jumbo shrimp
2 tbsp olive oil
2 cloves garlic, crushed
2 tsp ground cilantro (coriander)

FOR THE PICO DE GALLO:
3 large ripe tomatoes, deseeded and chopped
3-4 scallions (spring onions), white part only, chopped
2 jalapeño chilies, deseeded and finely chopped
1 handful fresh cilantro (coriander), chopped
1 lime, juiced

1 Clean and butterfly the shrimp. Mix together the olive oil, garlic and coriander and brush generously all over the shrimp. Chill until you are ready to start cooking.

2 Combine all the ingredients for the pico de gallo in a non-metallic bowl. Season to taste.

3 Either cook the shrimp on a barbecue, or on a heavy skillet over a high heat, until cooked through and a little charred. Serve with the pico de gallo.

First published in Germany in 2018 by Viking

Copyright © Viking

ISBN 978-1-909968-36-3

Book design by The Chelsea Magazine Company Limited

Photography: James Murphy
Additional images: AWL Images, Getty Images, iStock, StockFood
Recipe testing: Rebecca Wiggins

Printed and bound in Germany by Mohn Media

vikingcruises.com